This book belongs to:

____

24 23 22 21 1 2 3 4

Published by Tughra Books
335 Clifton Ave.
Clifton, NJ, 07011, USA
www.tughrabooks.com

ISBN: 979-8-89729-509-8

Mini Muslims Series ISBN 9781597849692

WHAT IS Salah?

When we pray to Allah it is called Salah.

Salah helps us remember and connect with Allah.

We pray 5 times a day.

In Salah we praise Allah and recite the Quran.

We stand, bow, sit, and prostrate.

Each Salah has a name:

Fajr, Dhuhr, Asr, Maghrib, Isha.

We love Salah!